CONTENTS

INTRODUCTION

2020 was a strange year. The Global pandemic caused swimming pools in the UK to shut and people to be locked away at home.

As the crisis was brought under control (for the first time) people were allowed out to exercise. For many swimmers this did not change their situation as the pools were still shut, but lakes, rivers and the sea were open and full of water, and swimmers need to swim.

After years of open water swimming and coaching I'd never seen so many people of all ages and abilities keen to swim in open water with organised sessions being oversubscribed and wetsuits quickly selling out everywhere.

Lots of the swimmers I came across were good competitive pool swimmers but had never swum in open water before. Their first experiences were mixed, some took to it like a duck to water and some were scared of the ducks in the water and wouldn't get in. All of them benefited from some basic advice and practical tips to make their swimming safer and more enjoyable.

I compiled a list of the tips and advice I'd passed on during open water swim sessions and arranged it into this book.

Swimming is a very personal experience; everyone has different thresholds for the cold or anxieties about being in open water. The tips in this book are very general in nature and should always be considered with regard to your personal disposition.

Most of the swimmers I work with are competitive pool swimmers looking to make a start or improve their open water swimming. This book is written with them in mind but the advice is equally relevant to swimmers of all levels.

I hope you find this a useful guide to help you get started swimming in open water and are able to put some of the tips into practice to improve and enjoy your time swimming outside.

DISCLAIMER

I have tried my best in writing this book to provide accurate up to date information based on current best practices. However, I do not take any responsibility for any errors or omissions, and I don't accept any liability for any loss or expense as a result of relying on the information contained in this book. You need to take responsibility for yourself.

Some of the risks involved in open water swimming are discussed in this book. I have only provided an overview of the risks of open water swimming and made suggestions of how to mitigate them. For more specific and personalised guidance find a qualified open water swim coach and discuss your situation with them.

If you have any pre-existing medical conditions seek medical clearance from your doctor before swimming in the open water and following any advice in this book.

The little book of Open Water Swimming

100 tips to get you started

PREPARING TO SWIM

1. Swim in a safe location

Finding a safe location to swim is important. Only swim where swimming is permitted and check local regulations if you are unsure.

Consider if the water is safe to swim in
- What is the water depth?
- Is there any visible debris in the water or obstacles?
- Is there any algae or other vegetation in the water?
- Are there likely to be other users in the water, boats, jet skis or kayaks

Consider if there are suitable facilities nearby
- Have you got a mobile phone signal in case of emergency?
- Is the site accessible to rescue services?
- What facilities are nearby? Is there somewhere to get changed and are there toilets nearby?

For your first swim in the open you may want to consider joining an organised swim and benefit from the experience of others in selecting a safe location. Remember you are always responsible for your own safety, so if you don't think it's safe, don't get in.

2. Check conditions are safe

Once you've found a safe place to swim you need to make sure the conditions are favourable and will remain safe for the time you are in the water. What is the water temperature? What is the tide doing? Is the weather expected to change? Is there a boat race planned on the river?

The experience of others who swim in your location can be invaluable here, as well as other users of the water who have already been in/on the water.

3. Plan your entry and exit

You are going to need to get in, and more importantly, out of the water.

Wherever you decided to swim should have safe entry and exit points. Imagine jumping into a canal with steep sides and no nearby steps or ladders it could be a long swim until you find a way to get out. River banks can also cause problems as plants or steep sides can make it difficult to get out wherever you want to.

As well as getting out at the end of the planned swim you may need to get out during so it's important to have exit points along the route.

Don't get in if you aren't sure you'll be able to get out.

4. Never go alone

Safety in numbers, no matter how good a swimmer you are never go for an open water swim on your own. If you get into difficulty and are on your own it may be your last swim.

You don't necessarily need to have another swimmer in the water with you, but someone nearby on the water who can help out is essential.

A friend who kayaks or paddleboards is useful to have with you, although they can get a bit smug if the water is cold.

If you can't find anyone to come in or on the water with you having someone on the shore is better than having no one, as long as they are able to stay reasonably close to you for the duration of your swim.

5. Use a tow buoy

Tow buoys are a very useful bit of kit for open water swimmers.

A tow buoy is simply a brightly coloured floaty bag that is fixed by a strap to the swimmer making them much more visible in the water.

Tow buoys should always be used when there are other users in the water you are swimming in. They are essential when swimming in the sea or rivers making you more visible to boat users. A tow buoy also makes it easier for people watching you swim from the shore to see where you are.

Some have waterproof compartments in them where you can store a phone or a drink and sandwich.

They can be bought online in a variety of colours for a much lower price than getting hit on the head by a boat.

6. Choose appropriate goggles, big or small, tinted or clear

Most open water swimmers are going to wear goggles, they are going to make it possible to keep the water out of your eyes and much easier to see where you are going, but had you thought about what type of goggles?

Goggle fit is obviously the first consideration and you need to wear goggles that are comfortable and don't let in water, chances are you'll have a pair from your pool swimming that work for you.

The lighting in a swimming pool is usually constant, whether it's night or day swimming pools are brightly lit. When swimming outside the light can vary, sometimes the sun can be low in the sky and swimming into it can be difficult, tinted or polarised goggles would be good if you are swimming in these conditions. On overcast days it can be very dark so clear goggles would be a better choice. You are definitely going to want clear goggles when swimming at night.

Some open water swimmers favour larger goggles which are like a halfway point between regular pool goggles and a diver's mask. The larger goggles provide better visibility and may also keep more of your face warm when swimming in colder water.

The choice on style is personal so try a few different types and see what you like best.

7. Wear a hat

A brightly coloured swimming hat should be compulsory for all open water swimming.

You want to be seen and as the head is the biggest bit of you that will be sticking out of the water why not make it as visible as possible.

Sometimes two hats are worn with the second hat going over the first and the goggle strap to help keep them on. This also keeps your head warmer than just wearing the one hat.

Neoprene hats can be worn to keep your head warm if the water is cold, but these tend to be dark colours so a brighter hat should always be worn on top.

Add a couple of extra hats to your kit bag so you always have a spare, there's always another swimmer who forgets or rips their hat.

8. Wear an appropriate suit, not too hot or cold

Knowing the water temperature before you get in will help you decide what to wear, you don't want to be cold but you also don't want to be too warm. If you find the water cold then a wetsuit should be worn.

There are lots of different types of wetsuit but one designed specifically for open water swimming is going to be best.

A good swimming wetsuit will be designed for maximum flexibility around the arms and shoulders and made with water repellent neoprene to help you glide through the water.

Tolerance to the cold is a personal thing, but I've listed some guidelines below for when wetsuits should be worn.

Below 15C (below 60F) Wetsuit and a neoprene cap
15-21C (60F-70F)   Wetsuit recommended
21-24C (70-75)   Wetsuit optional,
24C+ (75F+)   No wetsuit should be worn to avoid risk of overheating

If you are taking part in an organised swim or event they might have rules on what you must wear at different temperatures.

Always try before you buy, wetsuit fit is more important that brand name or colour and often price. A good fitting suit will keep you warm and make your swimming more enjoyable.

9. Wear sunscreen

Depending on conditions a sun block may be necessary. UV rays can penetrate the water so whilst enjoying a swim in the sun and you may also be getting burnt.

Look for a water resistant sunscreen with an SPF of at least 30.
Apply the sunscreen about 30 minutes before going into the water to let it dry.

Add some to your kit bag so it's there when you need it.

10. Be able to swim a longer distance in pool without stopping

If you are going to swim in the open water you need to be able to swim until you can get out, there is no rope or bottom to rest on.

When swimming in a pool you can't keep swimming in a straight line, you'll need to turn at the end and change direction, with a good push off the wall you may find only 80% of the distance you cover in a session is actually spent with your arms pulling you through the water, the rest is gliding away from a wall.

In the open water you are moving your arms continuously for the length of the swim, there are no walls for a sneaky rest, therefore you need to be able to swim a longer distance without stopping in the pool than you are aiming for in the open.

Conditions are also never usually as good in the open as they are in a pool, waves, swell and the wind can all make swimming harder work.

11. Keep hydrated

Drink water before swimming.

Most people will sweat considerably when exercising, but this can go unnoticed when swimming as you are already wet. (Try not to think of that next time you are in a pool). Studies have found elite level swimmers can sweat up to 1pint out during a 60 minute swim session.

You might feel cold when you first get in the water, but once you start swimming you will warm up and start to sweat; this is particularly true if in a wetsuit as they can do a very good job of keeping you warm.

Making sure you are well hydrated before starting to swim will help prevent fatigue, reduce the chance of cramps. You should also drink after swimming, you may not feel thirsty as you have been surrounded by water but it's important to get fluid back into your body.

12. Fuel for your swim session

You're going to burn up energy while swimming so you need to be properly fuelled to get the most out of your swim.

Don't have a big meal just before swimming, this may leave you feeling bloated and heavy and no one will be impressed if you are sick in the water. About an hour before swimming have some fruit or cereal or other fast digesting carbs.

Once you've finished swimming it's important to eat to fuel your recovery, have some carbohydrates as soon as possible but also add some protein in to help you recover. You can now buy recovery bars which make it easy to get the correct fuel as soon as you've left the water.

If in doubt have a banana.

13. Take dry clothes for afterwards

Make sure you have dry clothes to change into after your swim. An obvious seeming tip, but an important one.

Numerous times I've seen swimmers turn up for a swim already in their wet suit, they swim and get out and then realise that they have nothing to change into for the journey home. Whilst this is amusing to all the other swimmers, sitting in a puddle in the car on the way home is not pleasant.

For a more serious reason, warm and dry clothes are really important if you have been swimming in cold water, it's vital to get warm and dry as soon as possible to maintain your body temperature and avoid the effects of hypothermia.

14. Think positively

Think positively about your swimming. Try not enter the water with a negative mind-set.

Address any fears or anxieties you might have before you get in, talk to more experienced swimmers if you have concerns.

Watch others swimming to see how they prepare, the way they swim and the kit they are using.

GETTING IN
THE WATER

15. Know how to put your wetsuit on

If you are planning to swim in a wetsuit you'll want to put this on before getting in the water. Getting a wetsuit on can be trickier than you'd imaging and I'd definitely suggest having a practice at home before putting one on for the first time.

A good fitting wetsuit should be snug in all the right places, the downside of this means it will be harder to put on.

Make sure you aren't standing on any sharp ground that could tear the wetsuit.
Sit down if possible, but not on anything sharp.
Always pull the suit up using the pads of your finger-tips so the nails aren't able to rip the suit or wear gloves.

Put wetsuit on one foot at a time, point your toes and slide each foot fully through the leg of the suit, wearing socks or a carrier bag on your foot can help with this. Once one foot is fully out of the leg hole start on the other leg.
Next slide the suit up over your legs. Work up a little on one leg and then do the other leg so the suit is moving up evenly.
Once you have the suit to the waist check that that it is pulled up evenly over your legs and there are no folds, check both sides look the same.
Put the arms on one at time, slide the suit up the arm, once you have got one arm in and the suit is over your shoulder pull the whole suit up and then

repeat for the other arm.

Once both arms are in, try pulling the suit up further and check you have good flexibility across the shoulders. Smooth out any folds in the suit and make sure everything looks symmetrical.

I always get someone else to do my zip up for me, not only is it a good way to meet new people but it is better for the zip and they can make sure the cord is tucked away and any Velcro on the neck is done up.

16. Lube up when wearing a wet suit

I always advise swimmers to use lube when wearing a wetsuit. Lubricant is used to prevent chafing so should be applied around the neck, wrist and foot holes where the suit is likely to rub. I only ever get chaffing around the neck so only apply lube there nowadays. See what works for you, if it rubs lube it. Wetsuit specific lubricants are available but whatever you use it should be water based as petrol based lubricants will damage the wetsuit after prolonged use.

Adding extra lubricant to your arms and legs is a tactic often used by triathletes to help them get the wetsuit off after the swim as quick as possible.

17. Warm up on land before getting in

Before getting in the water it will be beneficial to do a quick land warm up if possible. The aim of this is to raise the heart rate and mobilise the joints to make your body more efficient and primed for the swim ahead. This shouldn't be too long or too strenuous; some of the exercises I like to use are listed below;

Arm swings - rotate one arm in a circle mobilising the shoulder joint. You can start with the arm held straight out to the side perpendicular to the body with small circles and gradually increase the size of the circle or just go straight into the full circles if you're more mobile; these have the additional benefit that you can check your wetsuit is on correctly and you have sufficient flexibility in the shoulders, do 10 about swings for each arm forwards and backwards

Jogging on spot – keeping the knees nice and high is always good for getting the heart rate up

Plank – if the ground is suitable holding a plank for a few rounds of 10-30seconds is a good way to activate the core

Press ups – again only on suitable ground, knock out a few sets of 5-10 press-ups.

Avoid doing too much land warm up if you are in a wetsuit as it's very easy to overheat.

18. Prepare to enter the water properly

Unlike pool swimming the water conditions can vary considerably when swimming in the open. It is important to get familiar with the conditions before setting off on a swim. If it's your first time open water swimming or you are in a new location or environment this will be especially important.

Have a good look around before you get into the water, do you know where you will be swimming? Do you know where the exits are if you need to get out?
Do the water conditions look safe? Consider tides, currents, algae, wildlife and other users as hazards.
Are you aware of the safely procedures in case you need to follow them?
Have you got all suitable kit with you?
For organised swims have you signed in?

19. Acclimatise

If possible get in slowly and carefully, taking time to get used to the difference between air and water temperature.

Splash water on your face then put your head under the water.
Float on your back to get used to the feeling of being in a wetsuit and the change in buoyancy and how you float.

Flush some water down the front or back of your wetsuit, it will initially be cold but your body will warm this water up and the wetsuit will trap it to keep you warm.

20. Avoid cold water shock

Cold water shock refers to the bodies reactions to being suddenly immersed in cold water.

These reactions happen subconsciously to protect us, but may actually do the opposite.

Sudden immersion in cold water can cause hyper-ventilating (rapid breathing) and an increase in blood pressure as the blood rushes deep into the body to keep warm.

If you have followed the acclimatisation tips and are wearing appropriate swimwear you can reduce the risk of suffering from cold water shock.

If you or someone you are swimming with gasps for air uncontrollably or changes colour when entering the water try and keep calm and get the breathing under control, move towards the exit from the water and get out slowly and get warm and dry as soon as possible.

21. Have cold showers or baths

For the more hard-core swimmer who wants to swim in colder water you can train your body to become used to the cold. There is an increased danger of heart attack or stroke when being subjected to cold water so give this a miss or at least talk to your doctor if you have any existing medical conditions.

There are actually loads of benefits of immersing yourself in cold water, but that's probable a whole other book. Look it up or take my word for it, it's worth doing.

The key to becoming used to cold water is to build up your tolerance slowly.

    i.   Start by having a shower as normal and then gradually lowering the temperature over a few minutes to as low as you can tolerate.

    ii.   Turn the temperature of the shower down as low as possible for the last 10 seconds of your shower, build this up until you can do 2 minutes in the cold before getting out.

    iii.   Over a few days lower the temperature of the shower when you get in until you can get straight into a cold shower.

Baths are harder to change the temperature of, but getting in a cold one or even adding ice will help you become tolerant of the cold water.

22. Check goggles before setting off

Before setting of on a long swim and while you are still near your kit bag, do a quick check of your goggles, put them on and put your head under the water, check they feel comfortable and are correctly tightened. There's nothing more annoying than being 10 minutes into a swim and realising you have put your old scratched leaky goggles on by accident.

23. Put you hat over your goggles

Many pool racing swimmers wear their hat over their goggle straps to reduce the drag from the goggle straps and keep them as streamlined as possible. This is still a consideration for open water swimmers, but a more important reason to wear a hat over you goggles is to keep them attached to your head so that you don't lose them.

Putting your hat on after you goggles will mean there is less chance of them getting knocked off by a friendly swimmer getting too close, or having them stolen by an angry duck.
I've never seen anyone have their goggles stolen by a duck but I did see a goose run off with a swimming hat once.

24. Have a warm up swim

Just like the land warm up the aim of the warm up swim is to get the heart rate elevated and to mobilise the body for more strenuous exercise.

The warm up swim should start slowly and build up to a faster pace before you start your main swim.
It's also a good time to check you are comfortable in your wetsuit and to get familiar with the water conditions.

The length of the warm swim up will depend on several factors including the type of swim you are doing and your age and fitness level.

Often in open water swimming the warm up swim is actually just the first few minutes of your swim. Take it easy to start with to get used to the conditions and prepare your body for the rest of the swim.

If you are racing you'll want to go fast at the start then make sure to have a warm up swim beforehand if available.

25. Know how to signal for help

The most common signal for help that is recognised by lifeguards, divers and many other water users is a straight arm raised up above your head with your hand in a fist and then waved from side to side like a car windscreen washer.

It's worth knowing this signal not only for when you need help but also so that you don't stop and wave to friends and accidently end up being rescued.

You should also be aware of any other signal and warning sounds that may be made. For example we typically use;

One whistle blast to get a swimmers attention.

Two whistle blasts to get a lifeguards attention.

Continuous whistle blasts to signal an emergency. Six blasts per minute is the international distress signal.

Some venues use air horns or sirens to denote an emergency. Make sure you are aware of local protocol.

TECHNIQUE TIPS

26. Adapt your stroke

As we've already seen there are a lot of differences between swimming in open water and in the pool. It may be necessary to make some changes to your stroke to swim your best in the open water.

The first thing you'll notice if you are swimming in a wetsuit is that you are more buoyant. Therefore the position you float in the water may have changed and you may find it's easier to move through the water as your legs are now floating nearer the surface keeping you in a more streamlined position.

You could be swimming close to other swimmers and around obstacles so your stroke needs to adapt throughout the swim.

Waves, currents and the general movement of the water will mess with your timing meaning it can be harder to maintain a textbook stroke than it is in a nice still lane of water.

Only make changes to your stroke where necessary to adapt to the conditions.

27. Faster arms

In the open water you'll normally want to swim with a slightly faster stroke rate than you would in the pool.

In the still water of the pool it's possible to have a long glide when your arm enters the water before you start the catch and pull. In the open you'll need to eliminate this glide and keep your arms moving continuously.

The moving water you are swimming through means that you'll lose momentum if you pause your stroke for a glide and may actually come to a stop in the water. There is also the risk you'll be pushed off course or another swimmer will swim on top of you if you aren't constantly moving forward.

28. Straighter arm recovery

A high elbow recovery is what is usually taught in the pool. The arm is bent at the elbow and the fingers move forward close to the surface of the water.

The additional vertical water movement in the open means that if you try and swim in this style, there is a good chance your hands will actually drag through the water on recovery which will really slow you down.
Your hands may also catch on a wave during the recovery which again will slow you.
The answer to this is to use a straighter arm for your recovery; this will keep your hands high and clear of the water.

Don't fully lock the elbow, aim for a straighter arm.
Keep your hand relaxed on the recovery but well clear of the water.

29. Don't kick as much, maybe?

The extra buoyancy you'll received from wearing a wetsuit will mean that you do not need to kick your legs as hard as you would in the pool to keep them up and maintain a good streamlined position in the water.

As your legs are some of the biggest muscles you have, and they normally don't generate much of swimmers propulsion, not using them as much should save lots of energy during an open water swim.

You might, however, still want to use your legs more than you need to for the following reasons.

    i.   You still might want to kick to help keep warm, the extra energy burn from kicking your legs will help warm you up if you are getting cold, even a short burst of leg kicking can be enough to warm you up.

   ii.   Kicking your legs keeps other swimmers away in a race situation, without your legs kicking it will be easier for people to swim over you.

30. Keep your breathing relaxed

Try to keep your breathing relaxed, good advice for swimming in both the pool and the open.

It's particularly important to maintain relaxed breathing in the open as you will normally be swimming for longer distances without stopping.

Make sure your breathing is under control before setting off on a swim if you have got into cold water. It will be harder to calm your breathing down once you are on the move, take the time to acclimatise.

Those new to open water swimming may be anxious and this may increase the breathing rate when they enter the water, a longer period of acclimatisation and warm up may be necessary to get control over breathing before starting a longer swim.

31. Exhale into the water

Another technique that should be used in the pool and the open is to breathe out whilst the mouth is under the water so that when you rotate to breathe you only need to inhale.

By doing this you will not need to spend so long turned to the side to breathe and can keep a stream-lined head forward position for longer.

Exhaling should be done in a nice controlled way. You can breathe out through either the nose or the mouth and start to trickle air out as soon as your mouth is in the water. The last bit of air should be breathed out as you start to turn to take the next breath in.

32. Turn your body to breath not just head

Remember that you should not be turning the head to breathe; you should breathe by rotating the body sufficiently far, whilst keeping the head in alignment, so that your mouth is out of the water enough to get some air in.

You are aiming to keep in a streamlined position for as much of the time as possible whilst you swim, this means keeping your body in as straight a line as possible from head to toes.

Turning just your head to breathe will throw you out of alignment and mean that you need to make other stroke corrections to counteract this.

Typically people will pull across the centreline of their body with their arms or kick out with their legs open to make up for the fact they are lifting or just turning the head to breath, both these things will slow your swimming down.

33. Breathe Bilaterally

Bilateral breathing means breathing to both the left and the right sides. It is a very important open water skill.

In the pool you can get away with only breathing to one side but in the open you need to be able to breathe to both for several reasons;

    i.   It keeps your stroke even and helps with swimming straight.

    ii.   To see were you are going. With no lane rope to follow bilateral breathing will help you check you are on course.

    iii.   If you are following a course marked out with buoys it is useful to be able to breath to the side the buoys are on which will be different if the course goes clockwise or anticlockwise. The same is true if you are swimming around an island or following the shoreline.

    iv.   You may not be able to breathe to a particular side because of waves or swell or the sun being low in the sky making it difficult to see.

    v.   You can keep an eye on other swimmers if you are racing or for safety if it's a social group swim.

Practice breathing to both sides in every training session, both pool and open water.

34. Breathe away from waves

If you try and breathe into a wave you are going to end up swallowing it, in sea swims make sure you are breathing to the side away from waves.

If there are safety boats or regular boats visible where you are swimming be aware that they can create waves. Jet Ski users are particular fond of creating waves near swimmers so make sure to watch out for artificially generated waves in what was originally calm wave free water.

35. Practice breathing with water in mouth

It's inevitable that you are going to end up with water in your mouth when open water swimming. If you don't swallow water when trying to breathe into waves you'll get splashed from other swimmers who you'll find yourself swimming much closer to than you would in the pool.

If you are uncomfortable breathing with water in your mouth it's worth practicing this to reassure yourself it's possible and you won't drown

The way you can practice this is to find some water you can comfortably stand in and then lower yourself straight down so that your mouth is half in and half out of the water, open your mouth so it half fills with water but continue to breath as normal. The cleaner water you practise this in the better.

36. Practice swimming in a group

Swimming close to other swimmers is something that many swimmers new to open water struggle with initially. In the open there is no defined swim direction like there is in a pool. Swimmers are also often not able to see under water so avoiding others becomes harder.

You will find you will not always be able to swim at the pace you want to as you may be boxed in by other swimmers or may be trying to keep with the group and not be left behind.

Your stroke will have to adapt when swimming in a group as there may be a foot or arm in your way preventing your perfect stroke.

It is worth spending some time practicing swimming in a group of swimmers.

Practicing in a group will help you identify if you are someone who is happiest out front leading and setting the pace, or following and relying on someone else to set the pace and the direction you are swimming in.

37. Test if you swim straight

When you swim in a pool it is quite easy to swim in a straight line, you can follow the lines on the bottom of the pool and there are lane ropes either side of you so you can't go too far off course.

In the open water there usually aren't any ropes to guide you and it's likely that you won't be able to see the bottom or maybe anything under the water.

A simple test to see whether you swim straight or veer to one side or the other is to swim with your eyes closed and see where you end up.

The best way to do this in the open water is to find a nice clear area of water with a fixed start point and a fixed point to aim at. If you don't have a fixed start point you could start next to a friend who will tread water in the same place while you swim.

From your fixed start point or friend, face the direction you want to swim in, aiming for a buoy or tree or church spire.

Close your eyes and swim 15-20 strokes in the direction of your aim point then stop.

Open your eyes and see where you are. If you swim straight you will be on a direct line between your start point and aim point, if you are not on this line you need to work on swimming straight.

This can also be tested in a pool, but take care to

avoid other swimmers if you swim with your eyes shut, it makes the lifeguards angry.

38. Learn how to swim in a straight line

In open water swimming you need to learn to swim in a straight line.

If you already swim in a straight line then you are good to go, otherwise there are some techniques that you can adopt to try and get yourself swimming straighter.

Make sure you are pulling equally hard with each arm and not more so with your favoured arm.

Keep your body straight by having a good alignment from head to toe. Everything should be and remain in alignment throughout your stroke.

Bilateral breathing also helps to even out your stroke as swimmers often pull in a slightly different direction on their breathing stroke. If you are always breathing to the same side you will always be pulled off course to the same side. The idea of the bilateral breathing is to even this out keeping you straighter.

39. Swim with crocodile eyes

Crocodile eyes are what we are aiming for when sighting to the front. A crocodile swims at the surface of the water with only his eyes peeking out and you should be doing the same.

Raise your head only high enough so you can see to the front. You only need your eyes to see so there is no need for any more of your face to come out of the water.

If you are lifting more of your head out of the water your legs will start to drop, this moves you out of a streamlined swimming position.

It is also more effort to lift your head to the front particularly when wearing a wetsuit so avoid lifting more than necessary to see.

40. Do not breathe to the front

You should not be breathing to the front when you are sighting. The actions of sighting and breathing are separate.

If you are breathing to the front you are lifting your head too high and out of a streamlined position. Sight to the front and breathe to the side.

There are 2 common approaches to this.

I.   Sight to the front and then turn the head to the side to breath
II. Turn to the side to breath and then turn the head back to the front to sight

Try both and see which method works for you

41. Push your lead arm down more when you are sighting.

When you raise your head to sight to the front you should be pushing directly downwards slightly with the arm that is extended out in front of you, this will help the head to lift and support your body so that you maintain your balance on the water.

42. Just a quick look not trying to see everything

When you are looking up to sight you should only be having a quick look. The sighting should not interrupt your streamlined stroke pattern.

If you didn't see enough have another look during the next stroke cycle, don't stop swimming to have a look around.

Try to have a reason for every time you sight, am I heading towards my next marker on the course? Are there any other swimmers in front of me I can catch up with? Are there any hazards coming up I need to avoid? Where's that scary swan gone?

43. Process what you've seen underwater

Don't spend time with your head above the water trying to work out what you are looking at, do this while your head is in a more streamlined position, with your face in the water.

Have a quick look up and then think about what you saw and if you are heading in the right direction, if you aren't sure have another quick look.

44. Kick your legs harder when sight-ing

The action of raising your head to sight will natur-ally cause your legs to drop lower in the water which will be taking you out of a streamlined swimming position.

If you find that you have to kick your legs harder to maintain you flat streamlined position most of the time then it's likely you are taking too much time over your sighting, remember it's just a quick peek.

45. Aim for visible landmarks

Pick something nice and big and visible to use for sighting. In-water buoys are useful but there also might be other landmarks that are equally visible, a distinctive tree or building, the top of a hill.

Whatever you pick to aim for make sure it isn't something that is going to move, using a boat to sight on when swimming in the sea would go badly wrong if the boat was moving.

46. Sight differently in rivers

When swimming in a river you need to take a slightly different approach to sighting.

Rivers have bends in them so you may not be able to see that far ahead of you in a straight line. Rivers also have banks on either side so you can use these for sighting.

In larger rivers, if you aim to keep a consistent distance from the bank all the time you will generally be following the course of the river and not need to sight looking forward for directions. By breathing to both sides you will also be able to check you are placed where you want to be in the river.

You should still be looking forward to check for obstacles and other hazards which may be in front of you.

47. Practice sighting in a pool

Sighting is a critical skill for an open water swimmer; as such you should be practicing it as much as possible.

It's very easy to practice sighting in a swimming pool, just have a look to the front with your crocodile eyes once a length during your training swims.

You should also be breathing bilaterally during your pool sessions and doing practice sets breathing exclusively to one side and then repeating for the other side.

GETTING OUT
OF THE WATER

48. Kick legs before getting out

The first time I raced in the open water I couldn't get out. I'd swum a mile course around a lake, worked really hard all the way round and finished strongly between the buoys marking the finish. Feeling good I swum straight to the shore and tried to run out up the slope. My legs wouldn't work; when I tried to stand up I just wobbled and collapsed back into the water. After a few minutes splashing around in the shallows I managed to stand up and get out. It wasn't until a few years later I realised what had happened at the end of that race and how lucky I'd been not to experience it since.

When you spend a long time swimming in a horizontal position and particularly when the water is cold and you don't use your legs much the blood drains from your legs to where it's more useful, the moving parts of your body.

When you try to move your legs again at the end of the swim the lack of blood moving through them makes then reluctant to work properly and very wobbly.

The advice is simple, as you come towards the end of your swim use your legs more to get the blood flowing.

A hundred meters or so before you have to get out start kicking more and maintain that to the end, even if you aren't involved in a sprint finish it's always nice to be able to get out of the water successfully with your dignity intact.

49. Use waves for a free ride to shore

Mostly only applicable to swimming in the sea, but take advantage of the waves.

As you are swimming into the shore catch a free ride on the waves, time your swim right and you can surf them into the shore fast and without much effort.

Obviously in a race keep swimming in, don't just stop and wait for a good wave.

50. Cool down swim

Before you finish a swim training session it's always a good idea to have a cool down swim.

Just as the warm up swim prepared you for the swim, the cool down prepares you for not swimming and starts the recovery process. You are aiming to slow your heart rate down.

Aim for a slower paced swim before you get out, with nice relaxed breathing.

If the water is cold just get out.

51. Avoid the after drop

The after drop is a dangerous phenomenon that occurs when your body continues cooling even though you are out of the cold water and starting to warm up.

While you have been swimming your body has cleverly moved blood away from the skin and extremities and keeps it in your core where it's easier to keep it warm and to keep you alive (thanks body).

It's important to keep your core warm when exposed to the cold as this is where all the vital bits for staying alive are kept.

When you exit the water your temperature will continue to drop even though you are out of the water and starting to warm up

If you warm up too quickly, by jumping in a hot bath or shower for example this can affect blood pressure and cause you to faint.

A good rule to avoid the after drop is to get warm as quickly as you got cold.
So if you were to fall in to some cold water and jump straight out you would be fine to jump in a warm shower or sauna to get warm. The body got cold quickly and for a short period of time so hasn't had chance to move the blood away from your extremities. Conversely if you have been swimming in cold water for an hour your body will be well down the

path of hoarding blood in the core and your arms and legs will feel cold, you need to warm up slowly to give the extremities a chance to get warm before the blood starts to recirculate.

The colder the water and the longer you are in it the more risk there is of after drop.

52. How to get warm safely

If you've been swimming in cold water you likely won't need telling twice to get warm when you get out. Even if you don't feel cold it is still important to get dry and start warming up as soon as you get out.

There are a few steps you should take to get warm efficiently and safely after an open water swim

I.   Get dry, get out of your wet clothes as soon as possible, even slightly damp clothes will really cool you down

II. Wear lots of layers. Silver foil blankets won't help as they stop heart escaping from the body and you won't be emitting heat after a swim.

III. Have a warm drink, heats up the body from the inside and is also tasty

IV. Have a warm shower or bath once you have started to warm up. Warm but not hot.

Think about how you are going to get warm before you get cold, it makes things a lot easier.

53. Log your swims

If you are interested in getting better at open water swimming it's important to track your progress.

Recording details of each session will allow you to assess how you are improving.
Logging how far you have swum and in what time gives clear proof of progress.
Also record any swim drills you did and make notes of things you need to practice in your next session.

There are various apps available for free to track workout sessions or a simple spreadsheet or notebook would do.

RACING STARTS
AND FINISHES

54. What are race starts like?

Open water swim starts are often messy; sometimes there are hundreds of swimmers all trying to get the best swimming line and fighting over the same piece of water. Sometimes a swim start is referred to as a washing machine as the water is so churned up.

If it's your first race, the best advice is to stay near the back and leave the more experienced to deal with the initial carnage, you'll get to swim in calmer water and chances are you'll use up less energy than those fighting at the start and overtake them later in the race.

If you want to start at the front you need to start quick, know which direction you are heading then put your head down and go for it. Ignore the 'nudging' from other swimmers that will be going on, kick your legs hard so no one can grab them and make sure your goggles stay on.

Things will usually calm down after the first turn when the pack will get spread out.

55. Learn a running entry

What could be easier? For a running entry you just run into the water and then start swimming.

If you've tried running through water you'll know that it's not too bad in shallow water but as the water becomes deeper it becomes harder, and running in water above knee high is not very fast.

To allow you to run further into the water you should keep your knees as high as possible and the use a running technique which involves turning the knee out as you lift your leg so that the leg goes over the water as you bring the leg forward rather than through it.

Practice starts before a race so that you can work out how many steps into the water you can do before you need to dive in and start swimming.
Also check the bottom for rocks or other sharp things before the race if possible.

56. Start like a Porpoise

Most often used for a beach start, porpoise or dolphin dives are performed after the end of the running start where the water is still shallow but not enough to continue running.

Once you have run in as far as you can you do a dive into the water hands first. The hands reach for the bottom and grab onto the sand or stones, they then pull back on the bottom while you quickly bring your legs forward between your arms. When both feet are on the ground between your arms you stand up and jump, diving forward into the water again looking to grab the bottom again and repeat until the water is too deep and you start to swim.

To someone watching you should look like a porpoise or dolphin gracefully leaping out of the water.

You'll want to have a look around the race entry point before you try this to make sure there are no hidden hazards under the water, diving into rock is not pleasant

Practice this lots until you are happy with it before trying in a race.

57. How to do deep starts

When starting in deep water you have nothing to push off from so are aiming to go from being stationary to swimming as fast as possible.

For either type of deep start you want to be looking towards the first buoy as this is the direction you want to move in, you also want to be horizontal in the water, as this is the position you will be swimming in.

For the first type of deep start you will be lying on your front, flat on the water, both arms are out in front of you sculling to keep you in position, your legs are straight out behind you flutter kicking gently.

When the start signal goes you will kick your legs hard and pull back with your favoured arm, straight in to front crawl stroke.

For the second type of deep water start you are lying on your side with one arm out in front of you but with your head still facing the first buoy you're aiming for.

Your legs will be performing a circular, breaststroke type kick; this can be done with alternating legs (egg beater kick).

On the start signal you will perform one big breaststroke kick and pull back with the arm that was out in front.

Try both start methods and see what works for you.

58. Practice starting from being still

There may be times in a race where you end up stationary in the water. This could be because you've had to stop to adjust your goggles or been squashed by other swimmers or a big bird is looking at you funny.

Whatever reason for stopping you are going to want to get moving again as fast as possible so it's worth practicing this in the open water or the pool.

During a swim come to a complete standstill (swimstill??) and then start swimming again as fast as possible using the techniques from the deep start.

59. Pontoon start

Starting off a pontoon is different to starting off a racing block.

Pontoons can be wobbly so take care not to fall in.

There are different methods of starting from a pontoon depending on the rules of the race you are in; if you aren't in a race you can just dive in once you've checked the water is safe to dive into.

    i.   Track start, similar to that used off a starting block with one foot in front of the other, favoured foot is over the edge of the pontoon ready to propel you forward on the staring signal.

    ii.   2 footed starts, both feet are on the edge of the pontoon with the toes curled over the edge. You can get 2 legs of propulsion off the pontoon for your dive in. This dive can be a bit precarious as pontoons often move in the water and swimmers jostle each other, only use if you are confident you won't fall in.

    iii.   Running start involves the start signal going off whilst you are a few meters back from the edge of the pontoon. On the starting signal you run forward aiming to get your favourite foot on to the edge of the pontoon and using this to power your dive into the water. This is also a technique used when re-entering water during a race.

60. Positioning for start

Positioning for the start is going to come down to several factors. If you get a choice think about the following;

I.   The swim course; consider the direction you will be swimming in towards the first turn buoy. Try to minimise the distance swum

II. Competitors; are there certain swimmers you want to swim in a pack with or some you want to avoid, position yourself near or far from them as appropriate.

III. Swim style; are you a fast starter who likes to get ahead and lead the race, or a slower starter who wants to avoid all the contact and jostling for position at the start.

61. Note where the swim finishes

For a swim only race find out where the swim race actually finishes. Is the timing stopped under a gantry out on the water or one on the shore after you've got out?

Valuable time can be lost if you stop swimming after passing the last buoy but the clock keeps running until you exit the water.

For triathlon and other multi discipline events make sure you know the event transition rules and route to be taken between race phases.

62. Swim until you can run

If the race is finishing on land, or you are transitioning to another discipline then you should continue swimming as shallow as possible until you are able to run.

In a reverse of the running start you'll want to be in as shallower water as possible before you start to run.

The knee turn leg flick over the water running technique can also be used to exit the water.

And you should remember to kick your legs as it approaches standing up time so they are nicely pumped with blood and ready to use.

63. Practice removing your wetsuit on the move

If you are in a race or an event in which the swim is only part of it and you are going straight from the swim to another discipline (running or cycling normally) take the time to practice removing the top half of your wetsuit down to the waist on the move to speed your transition in the next part of the race.

Make sure you can get hold of the zipper on the back easily and the zip is in good condition so the suit will unzip easily.

Keep your hat and goggles on as you unzip the wetsuit as that will leave both hands free to get the suit off.

Pull your arms out and slide the suit down to your waist as you run to the transition zone.

When you are at your bike or running shoes, give the wetsuit a good yank down and lift one of your legs up, this leg should come straight out of the suit, if it doesn't just roll the wetsuit leg down until the leg is free. You can then stand on the wetsuit with the freed leg and use that to hold the suit on the ground as you pull the other leg up and free.

This is a skill that needs practicing as you'll find what works best for you individually to get out quickly.

64. Customise your wetsuit

Triathletes will often remove up to a couple of inches off the legs and maybe the arms to make the suit easier to get on and off this should not affect the suits performance in helping you swim.

Try the suit on before making any alterations and make sure that it is fitting well and fully pulled up.
Note how much you want to cut off the leg and remove the suit.
It's better to cut off less initially and be able to take some more off later than to try and stick some back on.

Turn the suit inside out and using sharp scissors or a knife cut off the required amount keeping your cut parallel to the original finish of the suit.

Be aware that making changes to the wetsuit may invalidate the suit warranty, although some manufacturers provide explicit instructions on how to cut the wetsuit to avoid invalidating the warranty.

If you do decide to do this be aware you won't be able to return the wetsuit after shortening it, and don't do it to a hired suit.

RACING TURNS

65. Sight more on approach to turn

Sighting becomes very important as you approach a change in direction in your swim. Sight more on approach to a turn.

You need to be looking towards the buoy you will turn around but also at swimmers nearby to make sure you are in the best possible position to make your turn.

Don't slow your speed up as you approach the turn, many swimmers will and this can allow you to get an advantage, attack the turn as you should a turn in the pool.

It's also important to sight more after completing the turn to make sure you are on course for the next buoy on the course.

66. Kick legs harder as you approach and exit turn

Kick your legs harder as you approach and exit the turn.

You want to approach and exit the turn fast as this will give you an advantage over other swimmers who slow down and kicking your legs will help increase your speed.

Kicking harder will also help keep your legs up and counter their tendency to drop as you lift your head more to sight.

The other reason to kick your legs harder is to keep other swimmers away. The intent is not to deliberately make contact and kick other swimmers but to put them off swimming on top of you, forcing you under water.

67. Get in a good position before the turn

Just like the start of a race, turns can get messy. Swimmers are forced together and are all intent on getting in the best position in the water.

The best position to be in coming up to a turn is out in front, clear water ahead of you and you can choose the best line around the buoy.

If you are in the middle of a pack of swimmers the safest place to be is on the outside, it may take you longer to make the turn but you avoid all the jostling that goes on as swimmers fight for the inside line which should be quickest.

If you are in a pack try not to get stuck on the inside, swimmers in front will cut across you as they take the best racing line. There is also a danger of being pushed under the buoy if you are forced too close to it.

68. Arc turn

The simplest of all the turns you can do, you swim in a wide arc around the buoy.

This type of turn is best used when the turn you are making is very slight, for a very sharp turn you will need to swim in a very wide arc to get around the buoy and this will slow you down a lot.

69. Rudder turn

The next step up is the rudder turn. In this turn you will keep the arm on the side you wish to turn to extended out in front of you and do multiple strokes with the other arm. The extended arm acts as a rudder and guides you around the turn.

If you want to turn to the left, keep your left arm extended out in front pointing in the direction you want to turn, and then make as many pulls as necessary with just the right arm until you have completed the turn. Extend the right arm and pull with the left for a turn to the right.

Watch out for other swimmers when using this turn, as they may swim over your rudder, or be where you want to pull with the other arm making the turn difficult.

70. Corkscrew turn

The most technical of the turns you can do, but also the fastest for quickly changing direction.

This turn takes some practicing but looks impressive and is fast once you've mastered it.

To turn to the right, as you reach the buoy make sure your leading arm is the one nearest it (right arm). As you make a big pull with your right arm rotate to the left onto your back, make one backstroke pull with your left arm and keep rotating until you are back on your front and facing the way you want to go. To turn to the left lead with the left arm, rotate to the right and backstroke pull with your right arm.

If the turn you want to make is very sharp you can link 2 of these turns together, so you are rolling on your back twice.

I've found it useful to practice these on dry land first by imaginary swimming and walking up to a friend and turning round them. The hardest part is making sure you rotate onto your back in the right direction. Always rotate away from your lead arm, which is the one closest to the buoy.

DRAFTING

71. Draft as much as possible

Drafting is good; drafting can save you up to 30% of your energy.

Drafting is basically swimming behind another swimmer to take advantage of the bow wave or wake they create as they move through the water.

If you race in cycling you will be familiar with how much easier it is cycling behind someone else, the same is true in swimming, and it's also totally legal in all swimming races unlike cycling.

You will get a better draft following a faster or larger swimmer as they create a bigger bow wave.

72. Inline draft as close to feet as possible

An inline draft is simply swimming directly behind the swimmer in front.

When you are inline drafting you want to start as close to the feet of the swimmer in front as possible, without touching them. Ideally you want to be within 30cm of their feet, with your hands pulling in the bubbles their kick makes.

73. Arrow draft next to swimmers

The best position to be in to get a draft when swimming next to a swimmer is between their ankle and hip. In this position you can take advantage of the bow wave they are creating to save yourself some effort.

This is called an arrow draft, the lead swimmer can have 2 swimmers drafting of them, one to the right and one to the left, looking at them from above they will look like a triangle or arrow.

If you are no longer able to keep up with the swimmer you are drafting in this position you can drop back behind them and then try to maintain an inline draft.

You need to be especially aware and make changes to your positioning if you are drafting someone on the approach to a turn as it's likely the swimmer in front will cut across in front of you leaving you no room to turn.

74. Breathe towards swimmer you are drafting

You may think you'd want to breathe away from the swimmer you are drafting to avoid getting splashed, but you actually want to breathe towards them so that you can keep an eye on them and make sure you are in the optimal drafting position.

If you have a preferred side to breathe to, try to get in a position to breathe to that side while drafting.

75. Don't deliberately touch the swimmer you are drafting

Avoid touching the feet or hips of the swimmer in front, it will distract them and affect their rhythm slowing them down which will then slow you down as you are following them.

Touching other swimmers will also disrupt your own stroke rhythm and slow you down.

There is also the chance you'll get an 'accidental' kick to the face.

76. Stay focussed when drafting

Don't just blindly follow the swimmer in front. It can be all too easy to settle into a nice easy pace and cruise along not paying attention to anything other than the bubbles of the swimmer you are following.

Do not rely on the swimmer in front going in the right direction. Whilst drafting you still need to sight regularly to make sure you are on the course you want to be and have not been led astray.

You need to be especially aware and make changes to your positioning if you are drafting someone on the approach to a turn.

77. Match the speed of the swimmer you're drafting

Ideally when looking for someone to draft you want to find a swimmer who swims faster than you do. The efficiencies you will get from drafting will allow you to swim at a faster pace than normal.

Once you are drafting a suitable swimmer make sure you match their pace to maintain a good draft, you do not want to be dropping off their feet then having to race to get close enough again.

78. Break away if the pace is too slow

If you are in a race and are not familiar with the swimmers you are in the water with it can be difficult to know who you should try to draft off.

Be aware of the pace you are swimming at, if the swimmer in front slows down you may need to overtake them.

Unless you are out ahead of everyone else there will usually be swimmers further ahead that you may be able to catch up with and draft off.

Drafting is a good technique for saving you some effort, but you cannot draft all the way to the end of a swim and still win the race, you'll need to overtake at some point.

RACING DAY TIPS

79. Get there early

I always like to get to an event early, it gives you time to get all the admin side of the event out of the way so you can concentrate on your swimming.

Know what the check in procedure is before you get to the event, it's usual to have to register when you get there so the organisers know who is actually swimming on the day.
Is there any equipment that needs to be picked up on the day? Hats and timing chips are sometimes posted out in advance and sometimes handed out on the day.

Getting there early allows you to check out the facilities early so know where you can get changed and leave kit and where to check in for the start of the race.

There are usually several waves of races on a whole day event, so being there early will allow you to watch earlier races and see how the start and finishes work to get some tips.

80. Know the course

You may be sent a map of the course before the event, or the course may be revealed on the day you swim. Either way it's important to have a look at where you will actually be swimming before the start. Think about the following;

Will you be swimming around the course in a clock-wise or anticlockwise direction?

Are the buoys making the course visible? Are they different coloured to mark ½ way or certain distances on the course.

Where is the start and finish?

What position do you want to be in to swim your best race?

Sometimes there are many different distanced races swum on the same course so it's important you are aware of how your particular race is marked.

81. Hydrate & Fuel

Drinking and eating tips have already been mentioned but I'm going to mention them again in the race section as they are very important to having a good race.

Make sure you are well fed and hydrated leading up to the race but don't have a large meal and loads of water just before the race starts.

Have a good meal 2-3 hours before the start of the race; cereal, toast, baked potato, or sandwiches, something filling but not too heavy that is easily digested. 30 minutes before you swim you and have some dried fruit or a banana or an energy bar to top up your energy before the race.

Make sure to keep hydrated in the days leading up to the race, nice clear urine means you are sufficiently hydrated. Sip water until you are lining up to start the race if possible.

Practice your race day feeding and eating strategy before the race and don't try anything new on race day, a dodgy stomach halfway through a swim is not good.

82. Warm up

Another tip we are revisiting is the warm up. Warming up for a race is different to how you may normally warm up for a swim.

You are going to want to start the race fast so can't be using the first few hundred meters of the swim to get yourself warmed up.

Follow the tips for the land warm up if there is no in water warm up allowed.

At most events there is an area of water available for swimmers to warm up in, take advantage of this to get yourself warmed up and to get used to the temperature of the water and to assess the visibility under water.

Check your goggles aren't leaking and your wet suit is properly on in water whenever possible.

Try to warm up in water as near to race time as you can without missing the check in.

Make sure to keep warm or cool between warm up and the race start depending on the weather.

83. Take spare kit

Always pack spare kit as things often break at crucial times, take spare goggles and hats.

If you have different wetsuits and swim suits take those, conditions and water temperature can change quite quickly so it's best to be prepared for any eventuality.

84. Wear two hats

It's usual in organised races to be given a coloured and numbered hat to wear for the event. This may denote the wave you are swimming in or you age category, and it lets spectators and officials know who you are in the water.

These hats in my experience may not always be the best quality. So it's best to take a hat of your own to wear underneath the event hat if necessary.

85. Start fast

As we covered in the section on race starts, the start can be messy. If you are aiming to be competitive you will want to start at the front of the wave.

Aim to swim hard for the first minute or two until the race settles down and you can get into a good drafting position if possible.

If there is a buoy and a turn in the first few hundred meters of a race try and get there first as a lot of swimmers trying to make a turn at the same time is chaos.

If your goal is just to finish the event, keep out of the way at the start, you'll have a much more enjoyable swim avoiding the 'washing machine'.

86. Pace yourself

Open water events are usually longer distance swims so setting the right pace is a key element to doing well.

You'll hopefully have been training for the event and will know what speed you are comfortable swimming at and can maintain for the duration of the race.

Try to keep to your own pace and avoid getting caught up in the excitement of the race and swimming too fast too soon.
This happened to me in one of my early races, I got a bit competitive with some other swimmers early on in the race and paid for it in the later stages when my stroke fell apart and I had to be helped out of the water at the end.

Take advantage of drafting as much as possible but be conscious of the need to finish the event and if you are struggling to keep with the swimmer you are drafting with it may be better to slow your pace to one you can maintain.

87. Swim straight

With the invention of GPS tracking devices it's now possible to track a swimmer as they swim during an event. The results of this can be quite depressing when you realise that you have swum an extra 400m on what should have been a 2000m race because you did not follow the course as closely as possible.

Any improvements you make in your swimming technique or investment in an expensive wetsuit can be lost by swimming extra distance during the race.

> Learn the course
> Sight often
> Don't blindly follow others

TRAINING TIPS

88. Structure your training

If you want to improve your open water distance swimming the best way to do this is not to just get in and try to swim a long distance as fast as you can but to have a plan of what you want to achieve in each open water session, just as you should in the pool.
Split your training up into blocks with a warm up and cool down at the beginning and end.

Try sets of shorter distance swims but at a faster pace with a short rest in between swims.

As you won't have a big clock on the wall to check how fast you are swimming you may want to swim with a watch on.
You can also use stroke counting to break up your swim i.e. 30 strokes fast, 10 strokes easy.

Buoys can also be used to define the swim i.e. practice a start and swim fast until the first buoy, swim easy back.

89. Pace changes

Work on swimming at different paces during your training.
I like to split swim speeds into 3 categories;

Max Effort - The start and finish of a race should be fast, as should your approach and exit to turns.

Race Pace - Most of the race will be swum at race pace. This is the pace you can comfortably maintain for the distance you are swimming.

Easy – Slower more relaxed swimming speed used to warm up and cool down.

Make sure your training incorporates swimming at all 3 speeds.

Race pace is your most used speed so focus most of your time on swimming at this speed but don't neglect some max effort speed work.

90. Technical skills

Technical skills are very important in open water swimming and should be practised in every session.

Practicing technical skills can be incorporated into warm ups and cool downs, but it's also useful to have some specific time to work on skills separately.

You will always be sighting when you swim in open water but taking some time to think specifically about how you are doing it and working on your bilateral breathing will help you improve this crucial skill.

Spend some time doing short swims turning around a buoy in either direction to practice your turns.

Practice starts of each type and exiting the water, think about the technique you are using and how to improve it.

Get a group together and practice the different types of drafting, both with a cooperative swimmer leading and one who is trying to avoid being drafted.

91. Practice adjusting goggles in the water

Practice dealing with goggle issues as a part of your training.

If you are wearing your goggles under your hat as already mentioned you shouldn't lose them completely, but the jostling between swimmers that can happen in open water swims may mean they move and let in water or come out of position.

Practice draining water from your goggles whilst you are still moving as part of your training. This is easiest to do one eye at time and using the eye corresponding to the side you are breathing to. If you are breathing to the right drain the right goggle by lifting it slightly away from your face as your right arm comes past on its recovery, do the same for the left goggle whilst breathing to the left.

If your goggles are out of position you may roll quickly on your back and adjust them. An alternative method would be to lift your head to the front and reposition them with both hands.
Practice moving your goggles around in training so you have a plan of what to do if you need to make adjustments in a race.

Practice swimming with a bit of water in your goggles or with one eye completely filled up to get used to the feeling and to gain confidence that things are quite manageable even if not 100% perfect.

92. Practice swimming in a pack

Swimming close to other swimmers is something that I've found those new to open water can take a while to get used to.

In the pool environment we try and keep away from each other in a lane and swimming on top of people is frowned upon, in the open water you will need to swim near others to get the best racing line and to take advantage of drafting.

One of the drills I like to use to get swimmers used to swimming next to each other is to have 2 swimmers next to each other and have them match their stroke rates so their arms are synchronised and they are actually able to high five each other at the with the arms nearest each other at the highest point of their arm recovery. They then attempt to high five as they swim along.

Another more dangerous practice I use is to have swimmers follow each other as in an inline draft but have the swimmer behind constantly touching the swimmer in front's feet. The swimmer in front should try and maintain their stroke and not be put off by this.

93. Practice open water techniques in pool

There are several ways you can practice your open water techniques whilst swimming in the warmth and comfort of a pool.

If there are no lane ropes in the pool swim around the outside of the pool rather than up and down so you don't have to touch the end.

Sight to the front once or twice a length when you are swimming front crawl.

If there are a group of you swimming and you have a lane to yourselves swim lengths in a lane 2 or three next to each other, practice drafting in this way.

94. Make a cheap buoy

For practicing turns and sighting it's useful to have a buoy available to practice with in the pool.

You can make your own quite cheaply from a space hopper; get the kind with the loop handle rather than the original ear handles. Loop some rope through which is long enough to reach the bottom through the handle and attach a mesh bag to the other end of the rope. You can fill the mesh bag with weights and then position the 'buoy' hopper wherever you want in the pool, a lake or the sea.

95. Get someone to film you swimming

This is an eye opener for many swimmers, how you think you swim and how you actually swim can be two completely different things. By getting someone to film you swimming you'll be able to look at your own stroke and see if you are actually doing what you think you are.

If you can, be filmed in the pool and in the open, compare how your stroke is different, pull up some you-tubes of elite swimmers and see how you differ in what you are doing.

If possible get filmed from different angles, some things are better seen from the front or the side or even behind.

TAKING IT
FURTHER

96. Go to a coached session

Getting some expert coaching can give your open water swimming a real boost.

For those nervous about starting to swim an introductory coached session can help alleviate any worries you may have and give you the basic techniques and advice you'll need to swim safely.

More experienced swimmers can benefit from coached sessions to improve their technique. A good coach may be able to spot simple things that you've been doing wrong for years.

If you are a more competitive swimmer who races then coaches can provide advice on race specific skills such as starts, turn and drafting and also work on race tactics.

Group or individual coached sessions are usually available; just make sure the coach has relevant open water coaching qualifications and experience, and proper safety procedures are in place.

97. Join a club

There are now open water swimming clubs popping up all around the country as well as open water sections of 'pool' swimming clubs and triathlon clubs.

See what's available in your area and look at what's on offer. Some will offer coached session, some just a time to meet with other swimmers to swim.

Clubs may vary from the very competitive who train several times a week, to the purely social where every session finishes with a beer or cake.

As part of a club you may have more managed sessions available for you to swim at and a safer environment in which to swim.

Open water swimmers are quite a sociable breed in my experience.

98. Enter an event

Get a bit competitive, either with yourself or against others.

Enter an organised event; you can aim to complete the event in a certain time, to beat a friend or just to get round the distance.

Open water swimming events are run in the sea and in lakes and rivers; they cover all sorts of distances from 200m to 10km+.

Setting yourself the target of doing an event will focus your training and help encourage you into the water when you'd rather be somewhere warm and dry.

You also normally get a medal or a t shirt at the end.

99. Do an adventure swim

Adventure swims are non-competitive swims usually based around something interesting. They could be round an island in the sea, down a river or around a lake with stunning scenery. It would be normal for you to pay a company to guide you on this type of organised swim.

These types of swims might be challenging to do on your own where the benefit of a professional safety team or swimming in a group is necessary, they could be in hard to access locations or in areas where special permits are needed.

When looking for a company to book an adventure swim with check out their safety procedures. How much on water cover is provided? How big will the group swimming be? What are the swimming entry requirements, and do they look sensible compared to the swim being done?

100.   Go on a swim holiday

If you've really got the open water bug, why not book a swim holiday.

There are many companies now offering swimming based holidays, Global pandemics permitting.

Holidays can be anything from a few days of gentle swimming in a tropical location to a few weeks of long distance training covering thousands of kilometres a day in cold water.

Holidays can be boat or shore based with differing standards of accommodation to suit all budgets. Some offer video analysis and coaching to help you improve if you wish.

There are usually basic swim requirements before you can go on these holidays to make sure you can cover the daily swim distance.

FINAL THOUGHTS

Hopefully you've learnt something from this book and are now looking forward to your next or maybe your first open water swims.

If you're inexperienced or nervous try a supervised open water swim session or an introduction coached session. These are a great way to build confidence and understand the safety aspects of swimming in the open.

There are lots of open water swimming groups on Facebook where you can get information about swimming local to you. Most open water swimmers are helpful and welcoming but there is sometimes reluctance for people to share some of their hidden swim spots with strangers online to avoid the area becoming too popular and crowded thus ruining the magic of a peaceful open water swim.

You obviously have an interest in swimming and the open water or you wouldn't have bought this book and if you've made it this far and are still reading you've shown you are committed, so go outside, get wet and enjoy swimming in the open water.

Printed in Great Britain
by Amazon